ALLAH SPEAKS TO THE PROPHET MUSA علیه السلام

Quran Stories for Little Hearts

By
S A N I Y A S N A I N   K H A N

ILLUSTRATED BY CHITALI CHATTERJEE

Goodword Books Pvt. Ltd.
1, Nizamuddin West Market
New Delhi-110 013
Tel. 2435 6666, 2435 5454
Fax 9111-2435 7333, 2435 7980
e-mail: info@goodwordbooks.com
Website: www.goodwordbooks.com

Goodwordkidz
Helping you build a family of faith

About 3000 years ago, Egypt was ruled by a very cruel king called Firawn or Pharaoh.

One day a court soothsayer told Firawn that
that year a boy would be born among the
tribe of the Children of Israel who would
destroy him and his kingdom.

5

Enraged, Firawn ordered all newborn
boys of the tribe to be killed. The Children
of Israel, already enslaved by Firawn,
suffered the torment of seeing their
newborn sons killed, while only their
daughters were spared.

During these horrible times a pious woman, called Yukabid, of the Children of Israel, gave birth to a beautiful boy who was named Musa or Moses ﷺ. She was told by Allah that this was a very special child who would one day become a great prophet.

Allah inspired her to put him in a box, which she was to cast into the river Nile, with the promise that her baby would be safe. She obeyed Allah's order, and as the waves carried the box away, his sister kept a watch on it, until it stopped at a bank near the royal palace.

There it was picked up by a member of Firawn's household and brought to the queen. The queen was a loving, kind-hearted woman. When she saw the baby, her heart was touched and she exclaimed: "What a lovely child! Whoever sees him cannot but love him." Despite the king's objection, the queen decided to keep the baby in the palace and rear him as her own child.

13

The Prophet Musa عليه السلام, brought up with loving care by the Queen, received the best education.

But because Musa ﷺ accidentally killed someone, Firawn intended to slay him. Therefore, Musa ﷺ quietly left the city and journeyed to Madyan, where he met the Prophet Shuyab ﷺ and married his daughter.

After spending some years in the beautiful valley of Madyan, Musa ﷺ returned with his family to Egypt. They travelled slowly towards Mount Sinai, passing through awesome landscapes of desert and rock.

19

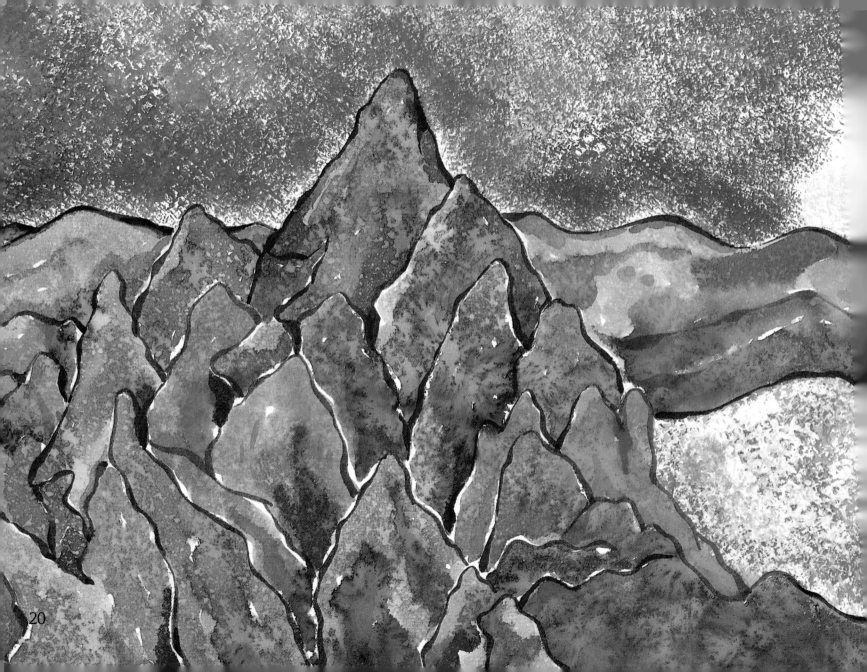

One cold winter evening, as it grew darker and a cool breeze began to blow, they seemed to have lost their way. Musa ﷵ looked around and noticed a fire quite far away on the side of a mountain. He said: "Wait here! Look, I can see a fire in the distance. Perhaps I can find out where we are, or at least get a burning brand to warm ourselves with!"

21

As Musa عليه السلام reached the source of the light, Allah spoke to him and gave him wisdom and miracles.

23

Allah told him that He had chosen him as His messenger and commanded him to go with these signs and give His message to Firawn, who had made himself a tyrant in the land.

Find Out More
To know more about the message and meaning of Allah's words, look up the following parts of the Quran which tell the story of the Prophet Musa ﷺ.
Surah Ta Ha 20:38-40, *Surah al-Qasas* 28:7-35

ﷺ *Alayhis Salam* 'May peace be upon him.' The customary blessings on the prophets.

24

Printed in India by NMIPL